MW00441979

A SWARM OF BEES IN HIGH COURT

A Swarm of Bees in High Court © 2015 by Tonya M. Foster
All rights reserved. Printed in the United States.

Second printing, 2020

ISBN: 978-0-9885399-1-4

Cover, interior design, and typesetting by HR Hegnauer.
Cover artwork by Wangechi Mutu, *Le Noble Savage*, 2006. Ink and mixed media collage on Mylar, 91.75 x 54 inches.
    Courtesy of the Artist. Private Collection, New York.
Page 123 artwork by Max Ernst, *Un essaim d'abeilles dans un Palais de Justice (A Swarm of Bees in the Palace of Justice)*, 1960.
    Oil on canvas, 51.6 x 77.25 inches. The Menil Collection, Houston. Photographer: Paul Hester.
© 2015 Artists Rights Society (ARS), New York / ADAGP, Paris

Belladonna* is a reading and publication series that promotes the work of women writers who are adventurous, experimental, politically involved, multiform, multicultural, multi-gendered, impossible to define, delicious to talk about, unpredictable, & dangerous with language. Belladonna* is supported by funds granted by the New York State Council on the Arts, Leslie Scalapino / O Books Fund, Leaves of Grass Fund, Poets for the Planet Fund, and from generous donations from our supporters.

State of the Arts

NYSCA

LESLIE SCALAPINO BOOKS FUND

Library of Congress Cataloging-in-Publication Data

Library of Congress Cataloging-in-Publication Data

Foster, Tonya
    [Poems. Selections]
    A swarm of bees in high court / Tonya Foster. -- First edition.
        pages cm
    "Distributed to the trade by Small Press Distribution"--T.p. verso.
    ISBN 978-0-9885399-1-4
    1. Haiku. I. Title.
    PS3606.O785S93 2015
    811'.6--dc23

                                2013011513

Distributed to the trade by
Small Press Distribution
1341 Seventh Street
Berkeley, CA 94710
www.SPDBooks.org

Also available directly through
Belladonna*
925 Bergen Street, Suite 405
Brooklyn, NY 11238
www.BelladonnaSeries.org

* deadly nightshade, a cardiac and respiratory stimulant, having purplish-red flowers and black berries.

A SWARM OF BEES IN HIGH COURT

TONYA M. FOSTER

BELLADONNA* 2015

"dust-nearing bees sink into the sanctum"
        —Zora Neale Hurston, *Their Eyes Were Watching God*

"one weeps because their body was the case"
        —Thom Donovan & Rob Halpern

It be…es that way, sometime

A mind is master
        but the flesh is boss—boned up,
        toned, taut or taught.

            A mind is.   Master
angels of incidence to
shake a booty down.

HARLEM NOCTURN/E/S

As always, there is
       our black robe.   Our tock-tock   clocks
            (y)our ga(i)t(e)s and g(r)avel.

               As always, there is
      this hill we climb—   (y)our thicket
of (st)roll and (st)utter.

As always, t/here *is*...
just *(i)/(u)s*. Was and will be? Y/Our
perennial (k)nots.

"As"—always t/here.   Is
unravel (h)ems of was/will
be(es), (h)is huhs, (h)er tongues.

IN/SOMNIA

Beside her, he lies
curled—sleeping apostrophe
—possession and "O!

      mission accomplished."
Again to t/his sweat. Now sleep.
But not for her—sleep

      less eyes like stagnant
city pools. Saltiness, then
this thirst for ice.

Another night's
gradations of darkness be
        come the counted sheep.

Another night's
darknesses like tar, like silt, like
steel wool coil along

her screen's narrow field
of light.   She wants to shout into
the pastoral sleep

of t/his face, to shout
at how sleep absents him, ab/dis
        solves him from/in

        to himself, *Pussy
is condition* −al, −ing, −er.
And position.

Chromosomal, pre
        positional.   Behind them
brackish water bangs

through bathroom pipes, through
the evening's tv tones,
through this cask of sleep.

Click the remote;
cough into the dark tree
of (y)our hands. S/w/allow

your voice back, into
the back/dark/spit of her throat.
Love's silence comes on.

Can running her
finger, like a hiss along
t/his clavicle trip up

parenthetical
affection? Full of sleep, this
dark husk pulls closer.

Catone and Cattwo
meow meeoows under
the closed bedroom door.

Unmet desire
ain't nothin' but a mother
of un/intention

as she stares into
her tv's 2 a.m.
glares, watches the way

she once watched
a boy's body—too quick for
caution and traffic

signs parse the asphalt.
Neighborhood boy, corner boy,
man to be—been. Bones.

Man to be—been. Bones.
Man to be—been. Bear this.
Man to be—been. Bones.

Done and *gone?*
What good is light on that?
To want and not ask.

To want and not ask.
To want and not ask to want.
To want and not ask.

She, in somnium
dramas, gets chased round the block
by rabid white dogs.

     She, in somnium,
     drums up the dreary, damned, stalks
     interstices 'cause

          "body" ain't only
          a grammatical sentence.
               There's no fleeing flesh

               with music so loud,
               and sirens, that you forget
               dis'quieting stars.

She's come to take this
as survival gospel
for sub'urban souls.

IN/SOMNILOQUIES

Earthworms aren't maggots;
eating them ain't planting a
tree or a flag,

she wants to shout at
her tv when some Sue gulps
earthworms from a cup.

She wants to shout at
this idea that there's p(l)ayback
for what's done/to come.

Earthworms aren't de'
composers nor dis'traction
from street corner noise.

You'd think a woman
would know this, she thinks. This thought
             a squirrel on a lawn.

You'd think a woman
             —there are thoughts of other women.
More squirrels.

Her mother: *I'd*
hate you to miss sex—when she
wanted to be a nun.

Her mother: *I'd*
like to hear this. What do you
know about a man?

when she wrote home about her lover whose mother taught her to knit.
When she wrote home about knitting, she was still girl-incognizant,

still the girl writing "we are the faces we wear." Where? In flashback,
still the girl with a face like a movie screen, who knit skullcaps with

yarn red as cartoon blood, as red as Mammy Two Shoes' shoes, matchstick heads,
yarn red as cartoon lips and tongues, red as bandanas and pomegranates,

red as blood butterflied across the seat and white of summer culottes,
red as blood that says woman, maybe mother, says watch and count,
red as velvety cakes she thawed and ate over two months mo(u)rning times,
red as velveteen curtains she wanted to drape around this moment,
red as morning, as bluster, as bluff, as the flat of offering plates,
red as mourning, as unheeded signal to stop, as sliced rare meat,
red as cherry now and laters, as pickled pig's lips, as bruised knuckles,
red as cherry blow pops, as big red gum, as loitering before sleep,

red as distant Red Hook bees drunk on cherry fungicide cocktails,
red as distant space mapped bought and belonging to brutish say-so,
red as the administration of districts and blocked-off blocks,
red as the administration of want, as the red-handed wave so long,
red as red squirrels, as maples, as districts set for and lit with wanting,
red as red squirrels—North American, Eurasian, native, migrant,

red, as red as red. Ass red as a baboon's ass is red. *Come on. Stop.*
...red as red-ass-red, as the seeping of coulda, woulda...you know.

Red as subjunctive being being the butt of taken and took down,
red as subjecting being's becoming to merchandising lines and limits.

A red-letter day in the red-light district of insomniac night,
A red-letter day for seeing red scare the shit out of reason—

red culled from rubia or madder root lends the hermit majesty, (the woman infamy),
red culled from sawdust of the brazilwood tree primped a pope's robes, pimped pus(sy),
red culled from clay, from crushed cochineal, kermes, from worms dried and ground,
red culled from cinnabar mined by the enslaved, the imprisoned, not-I's,

red as compass, gauge, as stripe, as strike, as undertone of home,
red as compass, gauge of light cycling the edges of 620 to 740nm,

red as was here, as becoming, as becoming not here,
red as note and gone and not...

each red a note the ear's noticing and gnawing, notational nothings,
each red a sheepish syllable counted in sleep's pursuit,
each red a sheepish syllable clocking the pursuit of shit,
each red a buzz, a buzz, a buzz, a buzz, a buzz, a blazon of want.

Color that
(the) temporarily color
            blind first perceive—red.

                Be utterly fly,
                swims through corner voices.
                To be is to be.

                            Be utterly fly.
                            Be itch, be road, be ache, be-
                                        tween want   have—reach.

Color that
dis'appears in early film—
black, boot-black, blue-black.

To see and to be
seen is what it is to live on
perennial blocks;

to see and to be
seen as somehow familiar
with all the look-backs.

To know... is to be
thought known. Friend A. says, "They see
my clothes, think I got cash."

be low be lack be ridge and grudge
be longing be sotted be ramble and hold
be come and go; be rim and ram the ball into the basket.
be ram-in-the-bush important
be stung be ache be ring
be reft and reach over
be attitudes of bee sting
be head nigger in changes of the light night's brigade
be moan and own ow!
below beehives, the haves' harvest
s/he be   tired

Look back at them;
see if they are looking back
at you and yours.

To know is to be a spoon in a kitchen drawer, wearing expertise.
To know is to be a spoon, bent burnt, crystalline skeins, shining held hollow.

To know is to believe.
To know is to be made infinitive—grammar and psychology.
To know is to be? This is a math of blood, a math of bodies, a (map of the math of bodies).

To know is to be conqueror, to be light infiltrating, descent.
To know is to be boundary, bounded—city/lover s/he'll leave.

To know is to become partial, to partition vegetables and fruit—
    To partition the s/he s/he might have become from the s/he s/he is,
    To partition the s/he seeing from the s/he that's seen, made up/over.

To know is to parse you from what you thought you were—my nigga is…
To know is to parse you from what you're told you are—my nigga that…

To know is to be inhabited—this cell of radiant waiting.

What s/he know 'bout
silence? How it settles in
a throat like *s/wallow*?

      How it settles like
      swallowing water or seeds
      they say might take root.

      How it settles like
      feet into the dailyness
      of their own falling.

What she know 'bout
be coming to mind at times
s/he thinks she don't think:

how her throat tightens like a branch on which cataclysmic swallows roost.

How her throat tightens tracks, through slow syllables, memory's algebra:

geometry of a park pool—a boy presses her twelve-year-old head—
geometry of an air-filled melon—beneath water with deft hands

she struggles against. Someone she can't remember sees her thin arms as
she struggles against his hands, their struggle breaking the water's skin.

As if to make plain the difference between a thought and a need,
as if to map the shifting climates between words and bare knuckles,

As if to show her knowing wasn't needing, he says he was playing,
his young voice filled already like a snow globe with the coming winters.

As if to show her the winters between words and his budding fists, he laughs.
His young voice fills all her thoughts of water, wades in each new syllable.

Yesterday swarms in
the m/arrow of (y)our thoughts (,/.) as
s/he lies t/here (,) sleepless

yesterday swarms in.
To eat or not to? Then what?
She clears her throat.

"You can't be eatin'
from everybody," her aunt warned
after the first loss.

"You can't be eatin'
like you don't mind trading a
baby for red beans."

That yarn's redness bleeds Persephone, Eve, Jemima, Rine. More squirrels.

(Amelia.Annie.Cardella.Noni.Butsie.BeBe.D
orothy.Althea.(Gwen.Akilah.)Jayne.Ai.Lucil
le.Ruby.Esther).

That yarn's redness: eating from a strange pot/tree/hand/mind draws blood or sleep.

Post-troubles—
Jemima was a daughter
of Job's winter.

Post-troubles,
Nancy Green plays pleasant aunt(y be)
                       fore a car kills her.

        How'd Job's Jemima
        become a handkerchief-headed
        pancake mix pimp?

        How'd Job's Jemima
        become aunty? "Jemima's *your*
        mama," she thinks/laughs.

This moment's the small
                 est measure of memory,
       cell of meaning.

This moment's "the small"
may, in a flash, be object
of central/forgot.

It was too late to
think about being (,) "got." No
good sleep in such thoughts.

"It was too late to"
was a slip of comfort; it
let such unrest keep.

But need is the swarm
                    ing of a sonorous and
deep-darkening hive.

But need is the swarm
that some women learn to feed
from their flesh of self.

Beside her, the dark
husk murmurs. What to do? Love
what could destroy you?

Beside her, the dark
　　　　　ness outlines low streetlight, these
　　　　　times, time again.

Beside her, the dark
husk murmurs in stereo—
chest, block, city, on…

Late night, commercials
with talk like urgent auctions
in uncrowded rooms.

Late night commercials
make her turn the tv down so
as not to wake him.

He's asleep
after telling her about the boy
he was, his father's fists.

He's a sleep
she can't fall to, a nap that
won't keep or unkink.

In sleep, his face distills,
his eyes unencumbered,
his mouth ridiculous.

In sleep, his face distills
the meanness of skin smeared a
                    cross bone and breath.

When Moses parted
the Red Sea as if it were
hair, was he tender?

When Moses parted
company with his crew, was
God at night enough?

Knots of a woman
who ain't numb with want. Who's not
effaced by shut eyes?

Nots form this woman
who sugars her mustards, who'll
want but never ask.

In her body swarms
swarms of cells, of tissue, of
sounds—"achoo," blood, "shush."

In her body, swarms
mundane sadnesses— wearied-
womb, "little cash," years.

Her self is a sleep,
is snake-eyes, knothole, whistle,
skull, gristle, and nerve.

Her self is a sleep
from which t/his voice might wake her.
To what? To what?

Black as tar. Black as
being. Black as boots, as
hollows, as (w)holes. "Your

black ass, tar black ass
know better," Cowboy's voice in
                    tones from livid stoops.

She wants a sleep
that shutters thought like the sparse
corner bodega.

She wants a sleep
shut against the neighborhood
graffiti of noise.

And Harlem, s/he can't
get the bedroom dark enough to
lose sight of things.

And Harlem, she can't
get tour buses of eyes to stop
trailing through her thoughts.

Blackity-black girl
sitting in a dark lit by
tv and streetlight.

Blackity-black girl,
at play on the court of (y)our skin—
eminent domain.

Voice of a woman on tv offers her sick roommate medicine.

Voice of a woman on a corner: "Stick your thumb up your ass. Smell it."

This hive of sound:
base-buzz, engine-crank. Voices laugh,
seal the sonic cracks.

This hive of sound
bruises her last 2 a.m. nerve.
"As if beats blind us."

AUBADE

As always, there is
the beat of siren and base
breaking the coarse dawn

As always, there is
some quadruped barking or me
                                owing light's hems

As always, t/here is
daily asphalt news (y)our
flesh and heat attend

As always, there is
a closed face watching from lit
& open windows

As always, t/here is
passage—door, street, gauntlet, be
                            fore, between, and then

As always, t/here is
love tossed among vials, spent shells,
t/his quiet leaving

As always, t/here is
t/his framed time—when we becomes
"I" among many.

How will more grief
enter his body? Malt liquor
into water goes.

How will more grief
be tucked away? "10% off"
and long check-out lines.

"Chivalry ain't dead,"
he says, holds open t/his steel door,
"just some of the men."

"Chivalry ain't dead,"
his Pops had explained, "and
it softens a woman."

On the stoop, Kim oils
his scalp, parts his hair into
tender paragraphs.

"On the stoop, Kim oils
and parts," a writer writes,
"her legs slash vulva."

Black is black taint
that marks the linoleum tile
she'll Mop & Glo clean.

"Black is black"—t'aint
that the color line—
"just cause" as refracted light?

Domestication
of need—*sage and lavender*
smoke out house spirits.

Domestication
of brush, of sweep, of scrubbing
and shine, of do and not want.

To be—the water
that bandies a body, the
body of a once

young wo/man on
a bayou of sound & words in
the pre/ab/sense of sleep.

To be—a boat as
in raft or pontoon. Each word,
a boat in which s/he

is, in which s/he is
sentenced and bandied about.
To be about to…

To be about…

To be bandied about by water,
to be busted and broke,
to be bored, grief-bore, work-bore.

to bleed,

to be backache, bone of nightshifts,
to be barren as salt lick, to bear bellyache and bloat,
to be news and less.

To be—tethered between seer and (un)seen.

To see and *to be*
seen?—what it is to live on
perennial blocks.

Her voice, no matter how loud or clear, is rendered silence, his do—
shadow projected across a page, across a street, an age, across
two bodies in bed.

BULLET/IN

Bullets can
pepper a body, like salt falling—
a startled cook's hand

        Rain, clear this
        Saint Nicholas hill, like a strong hand,
        of lean and wait

Bullets can
cover a street, a door, the distance
between yours and mine

        Rain clears this
        up—which is stronger—the grind of
        cars or cornered voices?

Bullets can
blot a page, train an eye to
follow thought and sound

        Rain, clear this
        moment's deadlock of was/will.
        Wash us in do/be

Bodies of young men—
spent smoke, spent casings graph one
among many points.

Bodies of young men—
site-specific installations—
streets, stoops, corners, cells.

They say "bitch" and mean
the syllable to break her
solipsistic strides.

They say *bitch* and *mean*
when she walks by seeming to
think thoughts blind to *them*—

block boys trying on
the tongues of the men they know
to be(.)Come cornered

block boys, trying on
these reins for y/our desires
—*bitch, chickenhead*

Don't think the body
don't think   the body don't think
   by feeling its way

Don't think the body
in its singular-plural
selves don't feel your gones

What doesn't kill her
maims her, makes her superwo'
        man (!) to be studied.

What doesn't kill her
right away becomes chronic
acquaintance until…

"I want that" becomes
her declaration of faith,
not in God, so much.

"I want that" becomes
how her soul hollers out: spade,
adidas, pumas.

"I want that" becomes
a way to clean the stench of
"ain't (got)," "can't (get)," "don't."

As if the soul could
be singled out from the cells,
from the room's clutter.

As is her soul wants
the solidity of the
shoestring, bean, or chain.

Justice — as a tally of things that can line a shelf or a closet.
Is it silly to say she is lonely? The city is ugly? She has failed?

She in the dark brick of a tenement building where brick trumps termite
She in the dark brick that won't trump rats, will trump decades but not roaches
She in the dark brick that is that which trumps flesh but not filth
She, in the darkening heat of a summer's meanness,
       —won't be persuaded by unnecessary beauty,
       —won't but believe brutality is how flesh understands:

    to shake or be shook down.

One she is no she to a me keeping tabs on the food money.
One she is no she, late evening, alone on a kitchen stool.
One she is no she in the dark air of her thirsty throat
             in the dank air of a dimly lit and distorting room. One window.
One s/he is no s/he. One is possibility only among many.

          One she is no she,
          not she enough to mark him.
          To see *her* is to see *them*—

     Yet one, not too many or more, is sufficient to count.

HIGH COURT

"If I was a bird,
I'd shit on you, and Keisha,
Chris, and Giselle too."

If "I" was a bird
instead of an axle-tree,
"we" might could fly.

We might could make
a plan, *make something out of*
apparently nothing.

"We-might" could make
I-am soar/sore, make "I" commit
to be an other.

Grammatical I
       ons: shit happens, shit be done
          happened, shit be.

Grammatical "I"
says, "Am." "Am." "Let." "Am I?" "I'ma
tell Mama." "I am."

Civil arrangements—
luscious grandmothers watch,
laugh from meager stoops.

Civil arrangements:
probiscus—blood, compass—field:
need's decorous courts.

Blind puddle that was
little boy's blood, cold water
and Mr. Clean clean.

"Blind puddle that was
chance for movie chivalry"—
                              sunlight dries this thought.

Blind-puddle-that-was
posit the boy, strutting man-
            to-be-been, the gones.

Blind-puddle-that-was
imagine sinews, tendons.

Tongue your wasness.

Blind puddle that was
miscreant affect of street-
                        side efficiencies.

Blind puddle, that was
his mama, cousin, grandma
weeping past your joint.

Urbanite widows,
you wear your mourning secrets
like tongues in closed mouths?

Urbanite widows,
wear your FUBU habits well,
mourning—routine bread.

B-BALL

Bounce-slap goes a ball
on a dark court. Hands, knees, and
feet clock slam and pass

       Steel comes in
       drum/strings his-her hands might
       boom/pling; gaze or spine

Bounce-slap goes a ball;
drilled-in-eye-dreams till concrete
with motion and sound

       Steel comes in
       these forms: blade, beam, molten, to
       feed, open, will, release

Bounce-slap goes a ball,
a hand. In memory, the
eye is quicker

       Steel come in, like a needle or love, like bodies
       of sound, of flesh, into

What becomes of the
in/aspirations? Sky-hook,
finger-roll, head-fake?

What becomes of the
swagger of faked-out jump shots,
cross-over dribbles?

His shoe will not grieve
the hand that held it, will not
want or want desire.

His shoe will not grieve
your hand's holding or its
shoeness when you're gone.

"I want to be like
Mike," says we, "want to wear his
skilled skin on my feet."

"I want to be like
Mike," say we, "just as long as
I can take him off."

Some "I's" want to bear
the beauty of LeBron down
to the shot and slash.

Some eyes want to bear
errant banners of burden
        less badassery.

SWARMS

With rained words, they make
merchandise of her in branded
pants, hats, cars, phones.

With reigned words, they make
a self he'll buy at discount/
markup,   depending.

Bent, brown body, your
bobbing head anoints pavement—
slight prayers like roaches.

Bent, brown body, your
bend, your bob under faint light
            —articulate bullets.

Tennis shoe pigeons
bounce, bend the cautious boughs, eat
wind with toothless mouths.

Tennis shoe pigeons
of our nature, mark now by then,
know *them* by profiles.

In the lit air above
and on broken concrete—un-
poetic pigeons.

In the lit air above,
pigeons wheel and hover, a
form in flight, not flight.

We understand light
within a form. The sand, or
water whipping it.

We understand light
we say because of what we
say: "flash," "blaze," "blind."

A bullet ain't got
no name, no neck, no notions
of right, time, or left.

A bullet ain't got
no address, no love, no need
for satisfaction.

HARLEM NOCTURN/E/S 2

As beings,   come,   dance
        each evening's fractal glitches.
Hear here,   hope's hustle.

As being comes dawn
        ing, each fearsome fucking glance
hacks into being(s).

"As"—always there. Is
unravel the (h)ems of was/
will be, (h)is huhs, (h)er tongues.

Not a, not the, not's
mouth/tongue, not-woman, not-man.
Not arcs circumstance.

Not a (k)not, the (k)nots
of certainty   drift   stain
court   hair ice s/kin us.

Not a. Not the. Not's
not (k)not. Not, knock(,)   O!pen this
(s)lumber of no sleep,

draw back the b(l)inds
which day to dailyness
maps over sense.

102

Draw back the blinds.
Bind bind and bound between teeth
of sleep, dream, tongue.

Draw back the b(l)inds.
Untie "boom" from car doors and guns,
days and market songs

Draw back   the   b(l)inds.
Drawback   what "just-looking" blinds.
Draw the b(l)ack that unbinds

is from always Is,
here from ancestral t/heres, know
from have always kn/own(ed).

Is "*from*" always
the cardinal hive through which our
looking flies?

Is "*from*" always
the lodestone which aligns/mis
          aligns meaning, love?

Is "*from*" always,
though in us, between us? The
sheets and shi(f)t(s) we t/read?

TO SHAKE OR BE SHOOK DOWN

Once as a girl, she dreamed an urban kingdom.

In the time of the dream, women of the kingdom were squatting over toilets, over gold chamberpots.

There was one man—he was understood as the king—in all the imagined city. And this "king" walked among the women and among the pots. The king checked and talked as he walked. He was saying much of nothing, checking to see what was in the pots.

Into the chamberpots, the women were defecating or giving birth. Some children, some shit. Some children and shit.

Copping a squat over a pot, she was one of the women, there in the kingdom, lined up along errant walls like tchotchkes, laboring away. (What is a kingdom if not a collection of things that one can arrange across a landscape or a room or a factory floor? An arranged cohort and lineage.) Constipated, she released neither a child nor shit.

The masses she felt inside her refused to be let go. And she refused to let them go despite not wanting to refuse, despite how much refusing hurt. This, one supposes, is desire. She cried about the lack of refuge, the lack of release, and still she held on because the hell that we know seems so much clearer than the unimagined heaven. And the nothing beneath her was cooling across her ass. She felt cool air passing in the emptiness of the pot. This is how what isn't comforts.

It was neither day nor night but she knew, in the way one knows in dreams, that she had been there a long time. And nothing came of waiting. Nothing came of hoping. And this nothing was the air that she breathed. And this nothing seasoned the eggs that she ate, the stew that she stewed. It slid so easily off the spoon when she ate. And this nothing knelt beside her when she prayed. Though seasonal, it squatted inside her like an old woman. This nothing buzzed loudly against her windowscreen at night as if it had to ask for entry, as if buzzing were sufficient language, as if the window were sufficient barrier. In and out were nothing.

As if nothing. It whirls about her house and head. Nothing kisses her, even when her lips are chapped.

Being, being be.

Being being,   being be.

Being being,   be

Being?   Being be
          hard on a body.   Be hard?

(Y)our body still breaks

open.

A GRAMMAR OF WAKING

1.

First, light

      commands   a dreaming

          eye   —open.

Against
this, the loud-when-hook-
          ing woman

draws her
Levolor blinds closed.
That, and look

     ing eyes
done dreaming. "Look back
     at them. See

if they
    are looking back at you."
(Radio

blink. A-
rhythmical.   Red.   Light.)
"Time to rise."

Sun, you
shine; little houses
draw your blinds.

2.

First light
           commandeers her dream-
                "I," and on

     St. Nick
     pavement, a deaf-mute
     draws his arm

     over
     his head—that bearded
     moon of no

     respite.
     (Ashy skin offered
     against light.)

     "Turn, face
     the concrete beneath
     you."   This is

     one more
     sky, close and someday
     covering.

     Tread light-
               ly in this parish
     of crevice

     and crawl.

3.

First light,
     ants, commas, doors, ears,
       "I," "O!" dream

punctuate
     her grammatical
        sky of sleep.

A voice
she dreams says, "Words are
much louder

than one
voice." Not enough to
     keep out sound

     and light,
     to keep from waking,
     to keep sleep.

Hungry
and articulate
syllables

     graze the
     field of this page.   Eat
     this bleached grass

                    and stone
                    and imperfect pitch.
Gobble

that first
articuation—
                        "Let there be

this…"   Re
                            make the sun his face
                            reflects (and

                        thereby
                        also his dark-moon face),
and the light

against
which she draws her blinds
                        (and thereby

                        also
                        her blinds, her hands, her
                        drawing shut:

her slight
shift of string, her slow
pull, her latch;

sky-turned
eyes, her iris, her catch
of breath, quick;

her shout,
mouth born of the
impossible

mouth made
of these syllables).

In quiet.

A GRAMMAR OF WALKING: BAREFOOT AND GRASS

                    To walk
        to have walked

                    to be walking in wake, in
                    sleep, in the sleeping

                    miles and stairs, "alone"—
                              a peninsular tragedy.
                              To bear and to bare

                                   (y)our body's pleasing
                                   and petulant weights; bone and
                                   flesh   just a flash. Walk

                                        the ground gently. Some
                                             day, it will hold you.   Blade,
                                   green blade, brown blade, dirt.

        What lies   to you   to me

        Some   day
        it will
        hold

NOTES: TITULAR LINEAGES

From *A Swarm of Bees in the Palace of Justice* to *A Swarm of Bees in High Court*

The vibrant chromatic chaos and the haunting title of Max Ernst's painting—*A Swarm of Bees in the Palace of Justice*—were two of the triggering tunes for this poetry. I first encountered the painting in the mid 1990s at The Menil Collection in Houston. For years, a small notebook carried the title and a small off-color reproduction of the work. I found myself turning, over time, to the question of how I might contend with Ernst's parsing of a visual field.

Several unfinished pieces were written as riffs off of Ernst's provocation. Some pieces and lines focused on "color," on relationships and hierarchies between and among hues. Other pieces focused on a sense of fragmentation evoked by the small two-dimensional areas allotted to each color on the broad field of Ernst's painting.

I had held onto Ernst's title and the small color copy for years, carrying them with me in my moves from Houston to Jersey City to Harlem, making notes along the varied ways of language, images, moments that seemed somehow related, seemed like green offshoots of Ernst's multifaceted title. At times, my notes, lines, phrases focused on the swarm, as collective or group or as mass, and, also, swarm as movement.

Bees are communal, plural, public, unindividuated, corporate, en masse. "Bees" triggered images of bees, of course. The bee also becomes s/he, syllable, sound—"b" and to be. I began to understand the problem of how to contend with the myriad impulses provoked by the painting as a problem of form. First, I changed the title. There are no surviving palaces or much talk of palaces in Harlem. There is a basketball court, where one might through practice and chops rule. There is constant courting on stoops and corners. There is the etiquette of courtship. There is the train to the courthouse. There are the nearby cops who card neighborhood congregants. There is the height of the hills, the height of the apartment buildings, the height of the cameras focused on streets and doorways and the small Saint Nicholas Park. There are myriad highs, highs from rocks, totes, and forties. High-tops hanging from phone lines. There is the high of the noisy and high-flying ghetto birds that flash their brights some early summer evenings. *A Swarm of Bees in the Palace of Justice* became *A Swarm of Bees in High Court.*

I began to think about and collect the language of the place—the people and things that occupy the place. This is a biography of life in the day of a particular neighborhood. The cameras, bodies, televised portrayals, voices, and doorways of the place demanded a different pronoun for dealing with the multiple as subject and as swarm of actors.

Central to this meditation—"We think, therefore we are t/here, therefore t/here is."

ACKNOWLEDGEMENTS

Many thanks to the generous editors and publishers of journals, magazines, and anthologies where versions of this work have been or will be published in print or online: *Litscapes: Collected US Writings 2015*, *boundary 2*, *The Recluse 4*, *MiPOesias—Quest*, *Free Radicals: American Poets Before Their First Books*, *Nocturnes*, *The Poetry Project Newsletter*, *POeP!*, *PennSound*.

I wish to thank The MacDowell Colony for support and time to work on this collection. Thank you to the New York Foundation for the Arts for a grant that was also a gift of time. Thank you to Jeffery Renard Allen and the Pan African Literary Festival for support and time to write in Ghana.

I would also like to thank the family, friends, and colleagues who offered generous help and support in the process of making this work. On the family front, thank you to Barbara, Chonda, Deanna, Briana, and Toni for real-world sustenance.

Thank you to the friends who read iterations and excerpts of this manuscript over the years: Marcella Durand, R. Erica Doyle, Jennifer Firestone, Rachel Levitsky, Brenda Coultas, Betsy Fagin, Jo Ann Wasserman, Leah Souffrant, Erica Hunt, Tisa Bryant, Alexis Quinlan, Ann Bogle, Laura Hinton, Brad Richard, Peter Cooley, and…

Thank you to friends who kept asking (for the manuscript, for work) and kept the conversations going, even when words seemed impossible for me: Belladonna* Collaborative, Rachel Levitsky, Daniel Machlin, Erica Hunt (sister from another mother), Leah Souffrant, Tyehimba Jess, Evie Shockley, Charles Bernstein, Rich Blint, and Sasha Dees.

Thank you to those whose work demands presence and response, those whose work is sustaining inspiration: M. NourbeSe Philip, Erica Hunt, Harryette Mullen, Aracelis Girmay, Juliana Spahr, Etel Adnan, Brenda Coultas, Joan Retallack, Fred Moten, Nathaniel Mackey, Kamau Brathwaite, Theresa Hak Kyung Cha, Amiri Baraka, Akilah Oliver, Wangechi Mutu, and on and on and on and on (till the break of dawn)…

And finally, thank you to those, who in the Fall of 2011, appeared in so many ways and kept me grounded and housed and fed and talked to: Barbara Foster, Chonda Coleman, Deanna Wright, Briana Trim, Ana Božičević, Erica Hunt, Leah Souffrant, Ammiel Alcalay, Aoibheann Sweeney, Frank Cioffi, erica kaufman, LaTasha N. Nevada Diggs, Tracie Morris, Brenda Coultas, Marcella Durand, Rachel Levitsky, Belladonna* Collaborative, the Poetry Foundation, *Tripwire,* CM, RZ, TB, TC, SJL, SP, AM, SS, NV, RE, MCH, AB, BI, SB, HR, TJD, ER, MZ, LGW, MD, BK, GO, JB, FR, MC, MM, CS, SG, MH, TS, DDP, RKE, LF, DP, RL, DG, IF, CE, PP, MY, JO, MB, DV, RL, FL, RL, FT, JS, EW, KL, ER, RA, CA, SF, RTM, DB, PT, JR, RH, KH, CF, DS, TW, EL, RS, LR, DB, ES, DM, FS, MH, EG, MA, and others whose names I don't yet know.

ABOUT THE AUTHOR

Born in Bloomington, Illinois, Tonya M. Foster is more accurately a native of a home that no longer is what it was (as always), a home made less familiar by time, by water, by natural calamities and socially orchestrated disasters. Home=New Orleans, or rather N'Awlins—that dike-enclosed fabrication caught among the Mississippi River, Lake Pontchartrain, and the Gulf of Mexico, three tongues that should dictate the wills and ways of the city. Now residing in Harlem, she is a co-editor of *Third Mind: Creative Writing through Visual Art* and a PhD candidate at the Graduate Center, CUNY, where she studies the poetics of place.

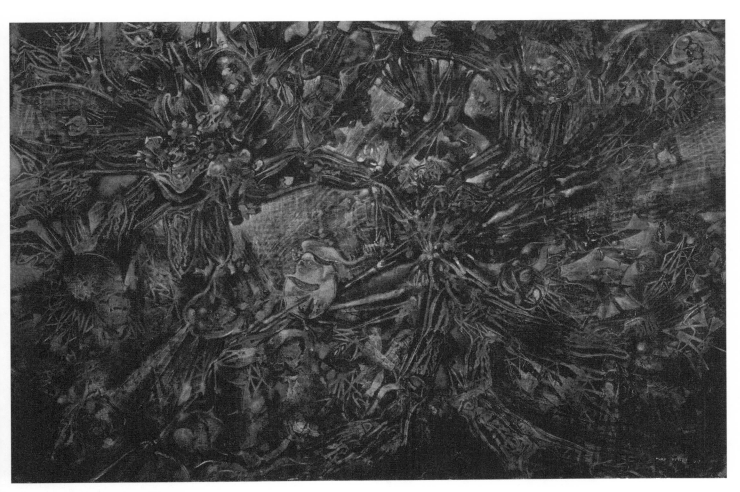

The Menil Collection, Houston